Roald Dahl's
REVOLTING
RECIPES

Roald Dahl's
REVOLTING RECIPES

Illustrated by Quentin Blake
with photographs by Jan Baldwin
Recipes compiled by Josie Fison
and Felicity Dahl

RED FOX

For Olivia and Lorina who both
died as a result of neurological problems. I hope the royalties
from this book will help others. F.D.

For Judith, with love; and for the
Neurology unit of Dundee Royal Infirmary. Q.B.

ACKNOWLEDGEMENTS

On behalf of the Roald Dahl Foundation, I wish to thank Quentin Blake for making this book possible by filling it with a feast of visual humour. A big thank you also to Josie Fison for inventing the wondercrump Revolting Recipes; Jan Baldwin, for her ingenious photography; Wendy Kress and Linda Ambrose for doing the typing while being force-fed the samples and suffering from constant indigestion; my editors, Tom Maschler, Melissa Jones and Clare Conville, and our designer Paul Welti for their constant faith in me. Last and by no means least, I thank Roald, my fantastic husband, without whose inspiration this book would never have happened.

Felicity Dahl. CHAIRMAN, THE ROALD DAHL FOUNDATION.

COOK'S NOTES

These recipes are for the family to enjoy making together. Some could be dangerous without the help of an adult. Children please have an adult with you when you are using knives, handling anything hot or using a food processor.

SUPPLIERS: We have tried to use ingredients that are available from your local friendly supermarket.

MEASURES: All measurements are given in imperial and metric. When you are following a recipe use either ounces or grams, not a mixture of the two.

A Red Fox Book

Published by Random House Children's Books
20 Vauxhall Bridge Road, London SW1V 2SA

A division of Random House UK Ltd
London Melbourne Sydney Auckland
Johannesburg and agencies throughout the world

Text © Felicity Dahl and Roald Dahl Nominee Limited 1994
Illustrations © Quentin Blake 1994
Photographs © Jan Baldwin

1 3 5 7 9 10 8 6 4 2

First published in Great Britain by Jonathan Cape Limited 1994
Red Fox edition 1996
This Red Fox edition 1997

Printed in Singapore

RANDOM HOUSE UK Limited Reg. No. 954009

ISBN 0 09 926307 6

Royalties from this book will be donated to The Roald Dahl Foundation whose aims are to help in the areas of neurology, haematology and literacy.

INTRODUCTION

TREATS

Treats were an essential part of Roald's life – never too many, never too few and always perfectly timed. He made you feel like a king receiving the finest gift in the land.

A treat could be a wine gum lifted silently in the middle of the night out of a large sweet jar kept permanently by his bedside. It could be a lobster and oyster feast placed on the table after a secret visit to the fishmonger, his favourite shop. It could be the first new potato, broad bean or lettuce from the garden, a basket of field mushrooms or a superb conker. A different kind of treat would be an unannounced visit to a school causing chaos to teachers and, I suspect, a great deal of fun for the children.

Just before Roald died, while we were writing a book about food we loved and happy memories, it was suggested we should write a book for children, based on the many wonderful and varied foods that appear in his books. Roald buried his face in his hands and gasped, "Oh no, Liccy, the work! The thought daunts me."

A few weeks later there, sitting on my blotter, was a pile of papers neatly clipped together, listing every food from Willy Wonka's Nutty Crunch Surprise to the mound of mysterious spare ribs consumed by Hansel and Gretel in *Rhyme Stew*. On top was a note saying, "It's a great idea, but God knows how you will do it."

Well, I *have* done it. *Revolting Recipes* is an interpretation of some of the scrumptious and wonderfully disgusting dishes which appear in Roald's books. Quentin Blake's part in all this is without parallel and his wickedly funny illustrations together with Jan Baldwin's skilful photographs and Josie Fison's interpretation make this book the *ultimate* treat.

Felicity Dahl, GIPSY HOUSE 1994

STRAWBERRY FLAVOURED CHOCOLATE COATED FUDGE

FROM 'CHARLIE AND THE CHOCOLATE FACTORY'

MAKES ENOUGH FOR 10 GREEDY CHILDREN

YOU WILL NEED:

8 x 10 inch (20 x 25cm) shallow baking tin
greaseproof paper
large saucepan
sugar thermometer
cutters

1 Line the tin with buttered greaseproof paper.

2 Put all the ingredients except flavouring and colouring into a large heavy-bottomed saucepan and place over a low heat.

3 Stir occasionally. Once the sugar has dissolved, gently boil the mixture and now stir all the time (to prevent sticking and burning on the bottom of the pan).

1 lb (450g) castor sugar (cane)
4oz (100g) unsalted butter
6fl oz (175ml) evaporated milk
a few generous drops of pink
food colouring
a generous ¹/₂ tsp (2.5ml) of
strawberry food flavouring
(Supercook)
4oz (100g) melted chocolate for
dipping

Place the sugar thermometer into the saucepan and boil to soft ball 118°C (245°F). This takes about 5 minutes.

4 Take the pan off the heat, stir until the bubbles subside and then add the flavouring and the colouring.

5 Beat rapidly with a wooden spoon until the mixture thickens and becomes granular, approx 3 minutes.

6 Pour the fudge into the lined tin and leave to set. If necessary, smooth with a palette knife dipped into boiling water.

7 With shaped cutters, cut out the fudge and dip one side into the melted chocolate; or decorate with piped chocolate creating different patterns as in illustration.

YOU WILL NEED:

2 large saucepans
food processor
sieve

1oz (25g) butter
12 spring onions,
roughly chopped
1 small potato, roughly diced
1 clove garlic, crushed
12oz (350g) frozen peas
1¹/2pt (900ml) chicken stock
salt and pepper

GARNISH:

6oz (175g) frozen peas
5fl oz (150ml) double cream

GREEN PEA SOUP
FROM 'THE WITCHES'

1 Melt the butter in a large saucepan.

2 Add the spring onions, potato and garlic.

3 Cover with a lid and sweat for 10 minutes.

4 Add the peas, stock, salt and pepper, bring to the boil and simmer slowly for approx 15 minutes.

5 Remove from the heat and liquidise.

6 Pass through a sieve into a clean saucepan.

7 Reheat adding the peas to garnish and cook until just tender. Add the cream and heat through, correcting the seasoning.

8 Serve in warm soup bowls with hot crusty bread.

WORMY SPAGHETTI
FROM 'THE TWITS'

SERVES 4-5

YOU WILL NEED:

2 large saucepans
food processor

SAUCE:

2 tbsp (30ml) sunflower oil
1 onion, chopped
2 sticks of celery, chopped
(optional)
1 clove of garlic, crushed
14oz (400g) tin of plum
tomatoes
1 tbsp (15ml) tomato puree
1 tbsp (15ml) parsley, chopped
1 bay leaf
1 tsp (5ml) sugar
2 carrots, grated
salt and pepper

2 tsp (10ml) olive oil
2oz (50g) fusilli col buco
spaghetti (curly spaghetti)
8oz (225g) tricolour spaghetti
(spinach, wholewheat and
ordinary)
6oz (170g) Cheddar cheese
(grated)

1 Heat the oil in a saucepan and sweat the onion, celery (optional) and garlic until soft.

2 Add the remaining ingredients for the sauce *except* the carrot, bring to the boil and allow to simmer for 30 minutes.

3 Remove the bay leaf and liquidise the sauce until smooth.

4 Return the sauce to the saucepan, taste for seasoning and keep warm.

5 Meanwhile bring a large saucepan of water to the boil, add the olive oil and salt, long spaghetti and then fusilli broken into thirds and cook until just tender. Drain.

6 Reheat the sauce and fold in the carrot until it is warm.

7 Divide out the spaghetti on each serving plate, spoon over the sauce and garnish with the grated cheese.

SNOZZCUMBERS

FROM 'THE BFG'

SERVES 8

YOU WILL NEED:

vegetable peeler
apple corer (round type)
paint-brush

2 large cucumbers
4oz (100g) tinned tuna
1-2 tomatoes, deseeded and
chopped
3 cocktail gherkins, finely
chopped
3 tbsp (45ml) mayonnaise
1 dsp (15ml) poppy seeds
salt and pepper

COATING:

a little extra mayonnaise
savoury popcorn
extra poppy seeds

1 Peel the cucumbers then, with the point of the vegetable peeler, cut grooves along the length of each cucumber.

2 With the pointed end of the vegetable peeler, at random, very carefully scoop little pits into the cucumber.

3 Cut off the ends of the cucumbers, about $1^1/_2$ inch (4 cm) and hollow out the seeds.

4 Hollow out the seeds from the body of the cucumber using corer, approaching from both ends, but keeping 2 inch (5 cm) of the centre seed core to act as plugs later.

5 Stand cucumber in a tall glass and allow the excess liquids to drain (about 30 minutes).

6 Thoroughly drain the tuna, mix in the chopped tomatoes, gherkins, mayonnaise and poppy seeds. Season to taste.

7 With a teaspoon fill the cucumber, packing the tuna mixture down with a teaspoon handle.

8 Replace ends, securing with previously made plugs.

9 Paint a little mayonnaise in the grooves on the outside of the cucumber and carefully cover with poppy seeds using a teaspoon. (A steady hand is useful!!)

10 Place a small piece of popcorn in each pit, putting a little mayonnaise in first to secure the popcorn. These can also be coated in poppy seeds if wished.

NB. There are many substitute fillings, ie taramasalata, cream cheese, smoked salmon and chives.

Sophie said the original Snozzcumber tasted of frogskin and rotten fish. The BFG said it tasted like cockroaches and slime wanglers. I wonder what you think?

FRESH MUDBURGERS

FROM 'JAMES AND THE GIANT PEACH'

MAKES 10 MUDBURGERS

YOU WILL NEED:

mixing bowl

1 ¹/₂ lb (700g) minced beef
1 medium onion, chopped
3 tbsp (45ml) tomato puree
2 tbsp (30ml) mild French mustard
1 tbsp (15ml) Worcestershire sauce
2-3 tbsp (30-45ml) capers, drained
4 tbsp (60ml) fresh parsley, chopped
salt and pepper
1 egg, beaten

1 In a mixing bowl, break up the minced beef.

2 Add all the ingredients, *except* the egg, and gently mix together.

3 Add the egg, binding all the ingredients together and pat into mudburgers.

4 Preheat the grill and grill for 4-5 minutes on both sides or fry in a non-stick frying pan.

5 Serve in a bun with a "revolting" relish. Cucumber relish is ideal!

ONION RINGS

(TO GO WITH MUDBURGERS)

YOU WILL NEED:

large polythene bag

1 onion
seasoned flour
vegetable oil

1 Peel the onion and cut into ¹/₈ inch (2-3mm) thick slices, against the grain. Separate the rings.

2 Put them in a large polythene bag, containing seasoned flour, and shake until the rings are lightly coated with the flour, shake off any excess.

3 Deep fry in hot oil until crispy and golden.

MOSQUITOES' TOES AND WAMPFISH ROES MOST DELICATELY FRIED

FROM 'JAMES AND THE GIANT PEACH'

MAKES 18-24

YOU WILL NEED:

food processor
cling-film
greaseproof paper
frying pan
kitchen paper

8oz (225g) fresh cod fillet,
deboned and skinned
2 tbsp (30ml) fresh ginger, finely
grated
10 spring onions, roughly
chopped
$^1/_2$ tbsp (7.5ml) cornflour
salt and pepper
1 egg white
6-8 slices of bread
(white or wholemeal bread)
sesame and poppy seeds
oil for shallow frying

These need to be refrigerated for 30 minutes before frying.

1 In a food processor quickly blend together cod, ginger, spring onions, cornflour and seasoning.

2 With the motor running add the egg white until just combined.

3 Spread the paste thickly onto the bread slices.

4 Sprinkle generously with sesame and poppy seeds. Pat the seeds into the fish mixture with the flat side of a knife.

5 Cut off the breadcrusts and cut the slices of bread into three equal strips.

6 Place on a plate with a sheet of greaseproof between each layer. Cover with cling-film. Place in fridge and leave for 30 minutes.

7 Heat a frying pan of oil until hot and fry the bread slices seed-side-down until golden brown. Turn over and repeat.

8 Drain on kitchen paper before serving.

BIRD PIE

FROM 'THE TWITS'

SERVES 4-6

YOU WILL NEED:

2 large saucepans
2-pt pie dish and a blackbird
(pastry funnel)
rolling-pin

$^1/_2$ oz (15g) pearl barley
1oz (25g) butter
1 onion, finely chopped
1lb (450g) turkey breasts cut
into thin strips
12oz (350g) pork sausage-meat
2 tbsp (30ml) fresh sage,
chopped (optional)
5fl oz (150ml) sour cream
5fl oz (150ml) natural yoghurt

1 Simmer the pearl barley in water for approx 20 minutes or until soft.

2 In a large saucepan melt the butter and gently fry the onion until soft.

3 Add the turkey strips and fry quickly until golden.

4 Remove from the heat and add the sausage-meat. Mix well.

5 Add the sage, sour cream, natural yoghurt, cornflour mix, chicken stock and beaten egg. Season and mix until all is combined.

6 Place the blackbird (pastry funnel) in the middle of the pie dish. Surround with mixture.

7 Sprinkle on the chopped ham followed by the chopped egg.

8 Preheat the oven to 200° C (400° F) gas mark 6.

1 level dsp (10ml) cornflour mixed with 1 tsp (5ml) cold water
3-4fl oz (75-100ml) chicken stock
2 eggs, one beaten, one hard-boiled and chopped
salt and pepper
2oz (50g) ham, chopped
9oz (250g) ready-made puff pastry
1 egg yolk
8 parsley sprigs with the leaves pinched off or
12 pipe cleaners (for legs) Dye the pipe cleaners with food colouring and singe the ends to look like toes (see illustration). Make this the day before.

9   Roll out the pastry to the thickness of a two-pence coin. Make sure this is large enough to cover the pie.

10   Cut a strip of pastry the width and length of the rim of your pie dish, brush the rim with egg yolk and press the pastry strip down onto it.

11   Brush the strip with egg yolk. Lift the pastry lid with the rolling-pin and lay it over.

12   Cut a slit in the centre and carefully ease the blackbird's beak through the pastry lid taking care not to stretch it.

13   Press the pastry down firmly onto the rim and cut away any excess. Crimp the edge.

14   Glaze the pastry lid with the egg yolk and scatter with pearl barley.

15   Use a strip of pastry for a worm, place inside the bird's mouth and glaze.

16   Place in fridge for ten minutes.

17   Bake in the oven for 30-40 minutes or until the pastry is well risen and golden brown.

18   Stick stripped parsley stalks in pairs into pastry crust to look like birds' legs. If you like, singe the ends of the stalks to look like toes. Alternatively use pipe cleaners as described above.

BUNCE'S DOUGHNUTS
FROM 'FANTASTIC MR FOX'

MAKES 12-14

YOU WILL NEED:

cling-film
two plain round cutters
(3 cm and 6 cm)
kitchen paper
small bowl

4oz (100g) soft brown sugar
2oz (50g) unsalted butter
1 egg
1lb (450g) plain flour
$^1/_2$ tbsp (7.5ml) baking powder
$^1/_2$ tsp (2.5ml) cinnamon
a good pinch of salt
2 tbsp (30ml) hot water
$^1/_4$ tsp (1.25ml) vanilla essence
4fl oz (75ml) milk
vegetable oil for deep frying
castor sugar for coating

These are best eaten warm. The dough needs to be made and refrigerated for two hours or overnight before cooking.

1 Cream the sugar and butter until pale and creamy – this can be done using a food processor.

2 Gradually add the egg until blended.

3 Add the remaining ingredients. The dough should be fairly stiff but smooth.

4 Wrap in cling-film and refrigerate for 2 hours.

5 Divide the dough in half and replace the other half in the fridge.

6 On a floured surface roll out the dough to $^1/_4$ inch (0.5cm) thickness. With the cutters cut out as many doughnuts as possible.

7 Gather up the scraps, roll and cut out as many additional doughnuts as possible and repeat with the remaining dough.

8 Heat the vegetable oil to 190° C (375° F) until it is sizzling.

9 Fry the doughnuts in small batches turning once until deep golden brown.

10 Drain on absorbent kitchen paper.

11 Place the sugar in the bowl and add a few doughnuts at a time shaking them in the sugar until coated.

12 Serve immediately.

THE ENORMOUS CROCODILE

Steps 1 – 7 should be done the day before.

SAVOURY CROCODILE

1 Slice one end of the baguette horizontally in half along one third of its length to make the mouth.

MAKES ONE CENTRE-PIECE

YOU WILL NEED:

wire coat-hanger (with hook cut off)
cocktail sticks
a long tray or board
palette knife

THE CROCODILE:

1 large baguette (body)
4oz (100g) whole blanched almonds (teeth)
14oz (400g) pkt of frozen chopped spinach (skin)
2 globe artichokes (scales and eye sockets)
1 slice of ham or tongue (tongue)
1 egg, hard-boiled (eyeballs)
1 black olive (pupil)
2 cooked sausages (legs)
12 cocktail gherkins (toes)

2 Now slice the other end horizontally to make his body leaving $^1/_2$-$^3/_4$ inch (1-2 cm) unsliced to make his neck. Carefully lift off the top of his body section.

3 Hollow out the top and bottom of his body. Then hollow out the lower jaw, leaving a wide border.

4 Insert his "almond teeth" into the border.

5 Fold coat-hanger in half and carefully place it inside his mouth to give the jaws support.

6 Defrost, drain and cook spinach. Set aside.

7 Boil artichokes for 30-40 minutes, drain and set aside. When cold, pluck off leaves, discarding hairy chokes, and keeping hearts (a treat for adults later).

FILLING:

(quantities depend on size of the baguette)
6-8 eggs, hard-boiled
salt and pepper
3-4 tbsp (45-60ml) mayonnaise
(Hellmans or homemade)
1 carton cress
Supercook white icing sugar

MAKE EGG FILLING:

8 Finely chop hard-boiled eggs, and season. Mix in the mayonnaise and cress.

9 Secure any loose teeth with icing sugar.

10 BODY AND TONGUE: Stuff the crocodile's body with the filling. Put in his tongue.

11 SKIN AND SCALES: Spread the cooked spinach over the body with a small palette knife. Mold the mixture to look like a scaley skin. Position artichoke leaves.

12 EYES: Cut the hard-boiled egg in half and turn the egg yolks round so that they protrude. Add the pupils (half-olives). Secure with cocktail sticks (as in illustration).

NB. IMPORTANT
This recipe is designed to create a centrepiece for a party or special occasion. If you wish to *eat* the croc – simply follow the recipe but do not insert the coat-hanger. His jaws will be closed but he'll still be delicious!

Warn children that there are sharp cocktail sticks in the crocodile's eyes

13 LEGS: Slice the sausages in half and position. Hold in place with cocktail sticks.

14 TOES: Add the cocktail gherkins.

GEORGE'S MARVELLOUS MEDICINE CHICKEN SOUP

SERVES 6

YOU WILL NEED:

large saucepan

*2 small or 1 large corn-fed
chicken total 5-6lb
(2.5kg approx)
4 small onions
4oz (100g) mushrooms
3 large carrots
2 leeks
3 tsp (15ml) tarragon
(if fresh, chopped)
salt and pepper*

If you want to serve this for lunch, you will need to make it the day before.

1 Quarter the chicken(s) and roughly chop 2 onions. Place the chicken and onions in a large saucepan and cover with water.

2 Bring to the boil and simmer until the liquid has reduced by half. Skim the surface when necessary. Top up and reduce by half again. This takes at least 4 hours. Cool.

3 Strain and reserve the liquid – you should have approx $2^{1}/_{2}$-3 pt (1.5-1.75l).

4 Pick the meat off the bones, chop and set aside. If you have time continue boiling the bones in fresh water, as in step 2, to add more flavour to the stock.

5 Chop remaining onions and other vegetables, add to the stock with the tarragon and cook until tender.

6 Season with salt and pepper to taste.

7 Before serving, add the meat and heat through.

26

KROKAN ICE-CREAM
FROM 'BOY'

This will keep for a couple of days before the Krokan begins to go soft.

1 Make the Krokan first. Lightly grease a piece of kitchen foil placed on a baking tray.

2. Mix the butter, almonds and sugar in a heavy frying pan.

3. Place over a moderate heat and stir all the time, taking care that it doesn't burn.

4. When it's a good golden colour, pour the mixture onto the greased kitchen foil.

5. Allow to cool completely.

6. Place in polythene bag and lightly crush into small pieces with a rolling-pin.

7 Soften the ice-cream and then stir in the crushed Krokan until thoroughly mixed.

8 Place the ice-cream mixture back in the freezer until it is frozen again.

TOFFEE APPLES

FROM 'CHARLIE AND THE CHOCOLATE FACTORY'

SERVES 4

YOU WILL NEED:

melon-scoop
orange sticks
(available at chemist) or
cocktail sticks
small saucepan
sugar thermometer
8 inch (20 cm) bowl containing
water and ice-cubes

These need to be made at the last moment because they will start to "weep" after an hour.

1 Using the melon-scoop, scoop out as many balls as possible from 3 apples. Each apple ball must have some skin on it.

2 Place an orange stick or cocktail stick into the remaining skin left on each ball.

3 Place all ingredients in saucepan and heat gently, stirring occasionally. Turn up heat and boil to 160°C (325°F). The mixture will become a deep chestnut brown. Turn off heat and allow bubbles to subside.

4 eating apples
$^1/_2$ tbsp (7.5ml) water
4oz (100g) castor sugar (cane)
1oz (25g) butter

4   Remove bowl of iced water from fridge. Working as quickly as possible, dip the apples into the toffee one at a time. Rotate a few times to get an even coating and drop into a bowl of iced water for approximately 30 seconds.

5   Now stick the baby toffee apples into the remaining whole apple and continue until all the toffee is used up.

HOT FROGS

FROM 'JAMES AND THE GIANT PEACH'

SERVES 6-7

YOU WILL NEED:

pencil
cardboard
pastry brush
pair of scissors or stanley knife
baking sheet

9oz (250g) ready-made
puff pastry
3-4 Granny Smith apples
(average size so when cut in half
they will fit inside the template)
1 jar of mincemeat or
6oz (200g) raisins soaked in
orange juice
1 egg yolk, lightly beaten with
1 tbsp (15ml) of milk (for egg-
wash)

The raisins will need to be soaked in the orange juice for a couple of hours.

1 Using your imagination, make your own template of a frog, measuring 5½ x 5 inch (13.5 x 13 cm) approx.

2 Preheat oven to 200°C (400°F) gas mark 6.

3 Roll out the puff pastry to the thickness of a two-pence coin.

4 With your template cut out as many frogs as possible, approx 6-7.

5 With a fork gently prick the frogs' bellies several times.

6 Cut the apples in half vertically.

7 With a melon-scoop or teaspoon, scoop out the core and seeds.

FOR EYES:

12 raisins soaked in orange juice

1 tbsp (15 ml) plain flour
1 carton of custard coloured with
a few drops of green food
colouring

8 Fill each apple-hollow with a generous teaspoon of mincemeat or orange-soaked raisins.

9 Egg-wash the pastry frogs using a pastry brush.

10 Place the apples cut-side-down on the belly of each frog.

11 Position their eyes using the 12 raisins.

12 Lightly dust a baking sheet with flour and place the frogs on it.

13 Bake in the oven for approx 15-20 minutes or until the pastry is risen and golden in colour.

14 Serve on a pool of warm green custard.

MR TWIT'S BEARD FOOD
FROM 'THE TWITS'

SERVES 4

This is an ideal time to use up all your leftovers, otherwise use the following ingredients.

YOU WILL NEED:

large oval plate

2 potatoes (large)
a knob of butter
a little milk
8 cocktail sausages
1 medium mushroom or ¹/₄ tomato (nose)
1 egg, hard-boiled (eyes)

1 Peel the potatoes, and cook in boiling water until soft. Drain and mash with the butter and milk.

2 Cook the sausages and peas and grill 1 mushroom, or if you are using a tomato for his nose, remove the pips and cut the flesh into a "nose" shape.

TO ASSEMBLE MR TWIT'S FACE

3 With a little of the mashed potato, form a base for his face on a large oval plate.

4 EYES: Peel the hard-boiled egg and cut in half, turn the yolk around and place on the plate for his eyes, add the half olives as pupils.

5 EYEBROWS: Cut his eyebrows from the toast (it is one continual strip as his eyebrows join in the middle).

1 olive, cut in half (pupils)
1 slice of bread, toasted (eye-brows)
1 medium sized mushroom cup, cut in half (ears)
6 small pieces of rolled-up bread or pine kernels (teeth)
matchstick crisps (bristles and hair)
Twiglets (bristles)
2oz (50g) peas
5oz (150g) baked beans
tomato ketchup
a little grated cheese
gravy (optional)

6   NOSE: Vertically cut the grilled mushroom in half and place on the plate as his nose (cut-edge-up). Alternatively use the prepared tomato.

7   EARS: Place half the mushroom for each ear.

8   HAIR AND BEARD: With the remaining mashed potato form a base for his hair and beard.

9   MOUTH: Join three sausages together, splitting them in half, but leaving his mouth corners attached.

10   TEETH: Use tiny pieces of bread rolled and pressed between your fingers into "teeth" shapes, and position in his mouth. Alternatively use pine kernels.

11   BEARD: Now build up his beard out of the remaining matchstick crisps (bristles) remaining sausages (cut into little pieces), Twiglets, peas, baked beans and tomato ketchup.

12   To warm up place in oven on 180º/190º C (350º/375º F) gas mark 4/5 for approx 10 to 15 minutes, or microwave (check manufacturer's instructions).

13   Sprinkle the grated cheese over his beard. Serve with gravy if you wish.

LICKABLE
WALLPAPER FOR NURSERIES
FROM 'CHARLIE AND THE CHOCOLATE FACTORY'

This wallpaper needs to be made a day or two before to allow it to dry out. This will keep easily for a week and can be rolled up.

MAKES 6 STRIPS

YOU WILL NEED:

food processor
small pyrex bowl
cling-film
rolling-pin
wire rack

5oz (125g) dried apricots
or 5oz (125g) dried apple chunks
¹/₂ tbsp (7.5ml) soft brown sugar
2 tbsp (30ml) water
1 tsp (5ml) powdered gelatine

DECORATION:

selection of fresh fruit
melted chocolate
writing icing
edible flowers

RICE WALLPAPER:

This is also delicious. Simply cut 2 sheets of rice paper into three 2 ¹/₂ inch (6 cm) equal width strips. Cut the other two sheets into three 1 ¹/₂ inch (4 cm) equal width strips. Centrally place the smaller strip onto the larger strip. Decorate!

APPLE/APRICOT WALLPAPER

1 In a food processor puree the apple chunks with the sugar, until the mixture resembles "chopped nuts". If using apricots, puree without adding the sugar and follow steps 5-9.

2 Put the water in a small pyrex bowl and sprinkle in the gelatine. Leave to stand for 5 minutes.

3 Now put the bowl on top of a small saucepan filled with a little simmering water and dissolve the gelatine.

4 Once dissolved, slowly add to the apple puree and mix well.

5 Collect the puree into a ball and place on a large sheet of cling-film, gently flatten with your hand into a "square".

6 Now place another sheet of cling-film on top and using the rolling-pin gently roll out into a thin squarish sheet about ¹/₁₂ inch (1.5 mm) thick (you should see through it when held up to the light).

7 Rest on a wire rack and carefully remove the top sheet of cling-film.

8 Stand in a warm place to dry out. An airing cupboard is excellent for this.

9 After eight hours or so turn over and gently remove the bottom sheet of cling-film and leave to dry again.

TO DECORATE

10 Cut each sheet of fruit into equal width strips and decorate with fresh fruit, melted chocolate, writing icing, edible flowers etc (see illustration).

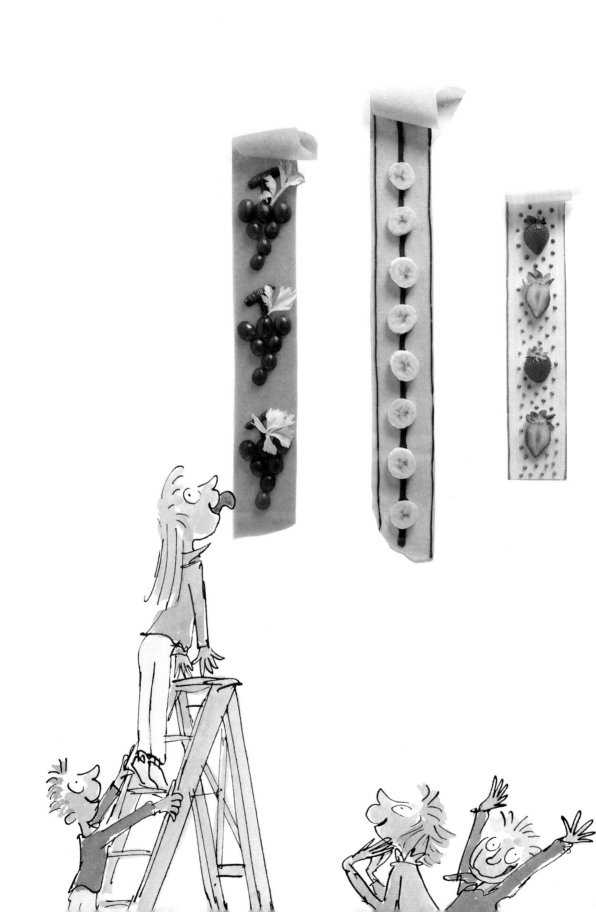

CANDY-COATED PENCILS FOR SUCKING IN CLASS

FROM 'CHARLIE AND THE CHOCOLATE FACTORY'

MAKES 6

YOU WILL NEED:

medium saucepan
sugar thermometer
8 x 10 inch (20 x 25cm)
baking tin, greased and lined
with greaseproof paper
buttered knife

6 pencils
play doh, plasticine or oasis
(available from florist)

¹/₂lb (225g) cube sugar
¹/₄pt (150ml) water
a good pinch of cream of tartar
a few drops of flavourings and
colourings

1 Put the sugar and water in a saucepan over a gentle heat and stir until the sugar has dissolved.

2 Raise the heat and when it's almost boiling add the cream of tartar and the sugar thermometer.

3 Boil without stirring to 121° C (250° F) .

4 Remove from the heat and add flavouring and colouring. Do not over stir and *be very careful* as the mixture is extremely hot.

5 Pour the mixture into the lined baking tin. The edges of the mixture will cool more quickly than the centre so, as the mixture cools, turn the edges inwards with a buttered knife, *but do not stir*.

6 Working quickly, lay two-thirds of a pencil onto the mixture. Lift up and gently turn the candy around the pencil. You can create all sorts of shapes but make sure the candy is almost set before you stand your pencils in the play doh, plasticine or oasis.

7 Try not to put your fingers on the candy coating as you will leave your fingerprints behind.

8 Repeat this with the other pencils.

NB. Do not double the recipe to make more, instead make in several batches.

HANSEL AND GRETEL
SPARE RIBS
FROM 'RHYME STEW'

SERVES 4

YOU WILL NEED:

roasting tin

1 ¹/₂ lb (675g) American style spare ribs
1 tbsp (15ml) Worcestershire sauce
1 tbsp (15ml) soya sauce
1 tbsp (15ml) English mustard (Colmans)
1 tbsp (15ml) tomato ketchup
1 tbsp (15ml) honey
1 medium onion, finely chopped
salt and pepper

1 Preheat oven to 220° C (425° F) gas mark 7.

2 Place the ribs in roasting tin.

3 Mix all the remaining ingredients together and with a knife paste the ribs with the mixture.

4 Place the ribs in the oven and cook for approx 1¹/₂ hours, turning every half hour, and basting them with the juices.

NB. These must be well cooked and crunchy, as in the picture.

BUTTERSCOTCH

FROM 'CHARLIE AND THE CHOCOLATE FACTORY'

*MAKES APPROX 1¹/₄ PT
(3-4 MUGS)*

YOU WILL NEED:

*large saucepan
large jug
whisk
cling-film*

*1oz (25g) butter
1oz (25g) castor sugar
1oz (25g) golden syrup
1pt (600ml) fat-free milk
3fl oz (75ml) natural yoghurt*

1 In a saucepan, over a low heat, melt together the butter, sugar and golden syrup, stirring all the time until the sugar has dissolved (about 10 minutes). Add a little milk to the pan, then transfer to a jug.

2 Whisk in a little more milk, approx 2 fl oz (50ml) followed by all the yoghurt.

3 Whisk in the remaining milk.

4 Cover with cling-film. Chill before serving.

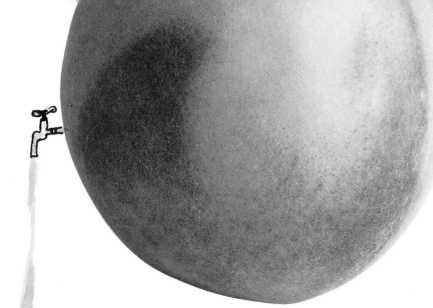

YOU WILL NEED:

food processor

14oz (400g) tinned peaches in juice
15oz (425g) tin mangos
1 lemon, squeezed
or
6 fresh peaches, skinned
¹/₂ mango (hairless variety)
1 lemon, squeezed

ice-cubes

PEACH JUICE
FROM 'JAMES AND THE GIANT PEACH'

Liquidise all the ingredients, add ice-cubes and serve immediately.

STINK BUGS' EGGS

FROM 'JAMES AND THE GIANT PEACH'

SERVES 4

YOU WILL NEED:

saucepan
bowl
sieve

4 eggs
3-4 brown outer onion skins or
1 tbsp (15ml) food colouring
mayonnaise
salt and pepper
2 carrots, grated
1 carton of cress

These need to be made a day in advance and can be dyed naturally or with a food colouring.

1 Place eggs in a saucepan filled with water and bring to the boil.

2. Gently simmer for 10 minutes, take off the heat, cool in cold water (this is important) and then drain.

3 Carefully crack the shells all over with the back of a spoon.

NATURAL COLOURING METHOD:

4 Put the onion skins in the saucepan, lay the cracked, hard-boiled eggs on top and cover with water. Bring to the boil and simmer until the liquid is a deep brown

colour, this takes approx 1 hour. Remove from heat. Now follow step 5.

FOOD COLOURING METHOD:

Place eggs in a bowl or glass, cover with water and add approx 1 tbsp of food colouring.

5   Leave to stand for at least eight hours or overnight before removing the shells.

6   Halve the eggs, press the yolks through a sieve, moisten them with a little mayonnaise.

7   The egg yolks can be mixed with a choice from the following; chopped ham, grated or cream cheese, chopped gherkins, Worcestershire sauce, curry powder, tomato sauce or cayenne pepper. Remember to season.

8   Replace the egg yolk mixture in the egg white halves and serve on a nest of grated carrot, and cress.

NB.   If you want to make the eggs very smelly sprinkle with ready grated Parmesan cheese or Asafoetida (obtainable from specialist Indian shops) which, smells like sweaty socks!

BRUCE BOGTROTTER'S CAKE

FROM 'MATILDA'

SERVES 1-8!

YOU WILL NEED:

8 inch (20 cm) cake tin
greaseproof paper
pyrex bowl
saucepan
skewer
wire rack
palette knife

8oz (225g) good quality plain
chocolate
6oz (175g) unsalted butter,
softened
8oz (225g) castor sugar
4 tbsp (60ml) plain flour
6 eggs, separated

COATING:

8oz (225g) good quality plain
chocolate
8oz (225g) double cream

1 Preheat oven to 180° C (350° F) gas mark 4.

2 Grease and line the cake tin with greaseproof paper.

3 Melt the chocolate in a pyrex bowl, over a saucepan of simmering water or on a low heat in a microwave.

4 Mix in the butter and stir until melted.

5 Add the flour, sugar and lightly beaten egg yolks.

6 Whisk the egg whites until stiff.

7 Gently fold half of the whites into the chocolate mixture, mixing thoroughly.

8 Then carefully fold in the remaining whites.

9 Cook for approx 35 minutes. There will be a thin crust on top of the cake and if tested with a skewer the inside will appear insufficiently cooked but don't worry as this is the character of the cake and it gets firmer as it cools. This cake is deliciously moist and light.

10 Leave to cool in the tin on a wire rack.

11 When cool enough to handle remove from the cake tin and discard the greaseproof paper.

12 In a pyrex bowl over a saucepan of simmering water melt together the chocolate and cream, stirring occasionally until the chocolate is fully melted and blended with the cream.

13 Allow to cool slightly.

14 The cake is prone to sinking slightly in the middle so place upside down for coating.

15 With a palette knife carefully spread the chocolate coating all over the cake.

16 Allow to set in a cool place before serving.

SCRAMBLED DREGS

FROM 'JAMES AND THE GIANT PEACH'

SERVES 2

YOU WILL NEED:

saucepan

1oz (25g) butter
2 eggs, lightly beaten
14oz (410g) can of chicken
consommé
salt and pepper

1 Melt butter in a saucepan.

2 Add the eggs and cook gently stirring all the time until the egg is scrambled and dry.

3 Pour in the consommé and heat gently, up to boiling point.

4 Pour into soup bowls and allow to cool slightly before eating. Season to taste.

NB. You can dilute the consommé with a little water if you find the taste too strong.

FROBSCOTTLE
FROM 'THE BFG'

MAKES 4-6 GLASSES

YOU WILL NEED:

food processor
sieve
large jug

8 kiwi fruits, peeled
1 $^1/_2$ limes, juice
8fl oz (200ml) lemonade
4fl oz (100ml) raspberry
drinking yoghurt
12fl oz (300ml) cream soda
1 tablet Redoxon
effervescent vitamin C (plain)

1 In a food processor, liquidise the kiwis with the squeezed lime juice.

2 Push the pulp through a sieve into a large jug (a few seeds will escape, this doesn't matter).

3 Add the drinking yoghurt and mix.

4 Gradually mix in the lemonade.

5 Finally pour in the cream soda and mix.

6 Let the children drop the Redoxon tablet into the jug. Watch and then serve immediately.

NB. If you wish to substitute drinking yoghurt with ordinary yoghurt add during step 1, when you liquidise the kiwis.
The kiwis may also be substituted with tinned gooseberries in syrup. (2oz (50g) gooseberries = 1 kiwi fruit.)
A drop of green food colouring will improve the colour.

CRISPY WASP STINGS ON A PIECE OF BUTTERED TOAST

FROM 'JAMES AND THE GIANT PEACH'

SERVES 16

YOU WILL NEED:

small round cutter
baking sheet
bowl

BUTTERED TOAST:

2 $^1/_2$ oz (60g) softened butter
$^1/_2$ tsp (2.5ml) cinnamon
4 slices of white bread

WASP STINGS:

2 $^1/_2$ oz (65g) shredded coconut
1oz (25g) icing sugar, sieved
3 tsp (15ml) clear honey/golden syrup
grated zest of $^1/_4$ of a lemon

1   Work the butter and cinnamon together until thoroughly mixed.

2   Cut four discs out of each slice of bread and set aside.

3   Spread 2oz (50g) shredded coconut onto a baking sheet and dredge with the sieved icing sugar.

4   Place under a hot grill until the sugar begins to caramelise (it will happen very quickly) then with a spatula turn over the coconut. Watch and repeat.

5   Place in a bowl and add the honey and lemon zest, and mix well.

6   Add the remaining coconut.

7   Toast the bread discs on both sides.

8   Spread with the cinnamon butter and top with the crispy wasp stings.

EATABLE
MARSHMALLOW PILLOWS

FROM 'CHARLIE AND THE CHOCOLATE FACTORY'

SERVES 10-15

YOU WILL NEED:

small and large saucepans
sugar thermometer
large heatproof bowl
electric whisk
15 inch x 10 inch (38 x 26 cm)
approx baking tin lined with
lightly oiled greaseproof paper
greaseproof paper
7 1/2 inch (19 cm) metal fluted
flan tin
4 1/2 inch (12 cm) bowl
cocktail stick or thin paint-
brush

MARSHMALLOW
PILLOWCASES:

1/2oz (13g) gelatine
3fl oz (75ml) cold water
13oz (375g) granulated sugar
6 1/2 fl oz (170ml) warm water
1 egg white, lightly beaten
1oz (25g) cornflour and
1oz (25g) icing sugar (mixed)
7oz (200g) mini-marshmallows
4oz (100g) icing sugar mixed
with 1tsp (5ml) warm water

This needs to be made two days in advance to allow the marsh-mallow to dry out.

1 Pour the cold water into a small saucepan. Sprinkle on the gelatine and set aside.

2 Place the sugar and warm water in a heavy-based medium saucepan and stir gently over a low heat until all the sugar has dissolved.

3 Bring to the boil and let the mixture boil to 118°C (245°F). Remove from heat.

4 Gently heat the gelatine over a very low heat, stirring until dissolved. Do not allow it to boil.

5 Pour into a heatproof bowl (rinsed out with cold water to prevent mixture sticking). Gradually trickle the sugar syrup into the gelatine mixture, whisking continuously with electric whisk.

6 When the mixture is well thickened, beat in the egg white a little at a time. Continue until the mixture becomes very thick, resembling thick meringue.

7 Pour the marshmallow into the lined tin and leave for 24 hours.

8 Dust a sheet of greaseproof paper with the cornflour and icing sugar mixture. Turn out the set marshmallow and peel off the greaseproof paper.

9 Place the mini-marshmallows on one half of the pillow-case and fold the other half over to encase them.

10 Seal the edges with glacé icing (icing sugar and warm water mixture).

THE FRILL:

1lb (450g) Regalice icing
1 egg white
writing icing
colourings of your choice

PILLOWCASE FRILL:

1 Roll out the Regalice icing to $\frac{1}{8}$ inch (2-3 mm).

2 Use the fluted flan tin upside down as a cutter to press out a circle.

3 Use your bowl to cut out a smaller circle and take out the centre, leaving you with a fluted ring of icing 1 $\frac{1}{2}$ inch (4cm) wide.

4 Carefully cut your ring into two halves and gently straighten out. As you do this a frill will form. Roll each frill gently with the end of the cocktail stick or paint-brush handle to encourage the frilling.

5 Repeat until you have the required length of frill.

6 Brush edge of pillow with egg white and very carefully attach frill, gently pressing down with paint-brush handle.

7 Leave to dry, occasionally lifting up the edges. It will eventually dry hard.

Your pillow is now ready to decorate. Pipe around the inside of the frill to neaten the join. Paint on stripes or pattern of your choice. The possibilities are endless!

BOGGIS'S CHICKEN
FROM 'FANTASTIC MR FOX'

SERVES 4-6

YOU WILL NEED:

large saucepan
large casserole dish
measuring jug

3¹/₂ lb (1.6kg) chicken
1 onion, sliced
1lb (450g) carrots, peeled and sliced thickly
2 sticks of celery
a few parsley stalks
salt
peppercorns
bay leaf
1 chicken stock cube
5oz (150g) peas

PARSLEY SAUCE:

2 ¹/₂ oz (60g) butter
2 ¹/₂ oz (60g) flour
³/₄ pt (450ml) milk
1 ¹/₂ pt (900ml) chicken stock

1 Put the chicken into a large saucepan with all the ingredients except the peas.

2 Cover three quarters of the chicken with water. Cover with a tight-fitting lid.

3 Bring to the boil, reduce the heat and simmer gently for 1¹/₂ hours or until the chicken is cooked.

4 Remove the chicken from the saucepan and allow to cool. Strain the stock.

5 Pick out the carrots and put to one side.

6 Skim off all the fat from the stock and put 1¹/₂pt (900ml) into a measuring jug.

7 Remove the flesh from the chicken carcass, discard the skin and chop up.

THE PARSLEY SAUCE:

8 In an ovenproof casserole or a large saucepan, melt the butter and add the flour. Stir and cook for 1 minute.

9 Gradually add the combined milk and chicken stock. Bring to the boil stirring continuously for 1 minute and remove from the heat. Add 5¹/₂ tsp parsley.

6 tbsp (90ml) chopped parsley
salt and pepper

DUMPLINGS:

4oz (100g) self-raising flour
2oz (50g) suet
2oz (50g) sweetcorn (optional)
cold water to bind
salt and pepper

THE DUMPLINGS:

10   Mix together the flour, suet, optional sweetcorn, and seasoning to taste. Bind with enough cold water to make a smooth dough. With floured hands, divide the dough into 12 portions and roll into balls.

11   Bring the sauce back to the simmer and add the chicken pieces, carrots, peas and the dumplings (they will sink, but don't worry).

12   Cover with a lid and allow to cook for about 20 minutes until the dumplings are light and fluffy.

13   Sprinkle with remaining parsley and serve.

NB. As an alternative to dumplings, you can make molehills out of mashed potato.

STICKJAW
FOR TALKATIVE PARENTS
FROM 'CHARLIE AND THE CHOCOLATE FACTORY'

SERVES 10-12

YOU WILL NEED:

piping bag and nozzle
baking sheet lined with bakewell
paper
wire rack

2 egg whites
a pinch of salt
4oz (100g) sugar
1 pkt old-fashioned treacle
toffees (eg Harrogate toffees
or any other hard toffee sweet)
with wrappers removed
food colouring

1 Preheat oven to 140° C (250° F) gas mark 1.

2 Whisk the egg whites and salt to the texture of stiff snow.

3 Then gradually whisk in the sugar until the mixture is very stiff and shiny.

4 Place the meringue mixture into the piping bag with nozzle.

5 Pipe a little meringue onto the lined sheet. Rest a toffee on top and continue to pipe as you would for an ordinary meringue making sure that each toffee is well-covered.

6 Repeat until all the meringue is used up.

7 Bake for approx 1 hour until dry and crisp and then cool on a wire rack.

NB. You can colour the meringue by adding a few drops of food colouring when whisking in the last amount of sugar.

WONKA'S
NUTTY CRUNCH SURPRISE
FROM 'CHARLIE AND THE CHOCOLATE FACTORY'

YOU WILL NEED:

pyrex bowl
saucepan
8 x 10 inch (20 x 25 cm)
shallow tin, greased and lined
with greaseproof paper
greaseproof paper

7oz (200g) plain chocolate,
broken into small pieces
2oz (50g) butter
5 tbsp (75ml) golden syrup
6oz (175g) Rich Tea biscuits,
finely crushed
3oz (75g) flaked almonds
1oz (25g) Rice Crispies
a few drops of vanilla essence

FOR THE NUTTY
CRUNCH:

2oz (50g) flaked almonds, finely
chopped
4oz (100g) granulated sugar
(cane)
2tbsp (30ml) water

1 Put the chocolate, butter and golden syrup in a pyrex bowl and place over a saucepan of simmering water. Stir occasionally until melted. Alternatively place in microwave oven and cook on high for 1^1/$_2$ minutes.

2 Add the almonds, crushed biscuits, Rice Crispies and vanilla essence and mix well.

3 Spoon the mixture into the lined tin and press down firmly with the back of a fork, creating a level surface.

4 Allow to cool in the fridge, then cut into bars.

5 Then make the nutty crunch; begin by placing the water and sugar into a small saucepan. Leave on a low heat until the sugar has dissolved. Do not stir, but occasionally swirl the pan around gently. Increase the heat and continue stirring until the sugar caramelizes and turns golden brown, approx 2-3 minutes.

6 Remove from the heat, add the chopped almonds, and working quickly, stir thoroughly and dip one end of the bars in the mixture. Place the bars on a sheet of buttered greaseproof paper to set.

7 Melt the chocolate in the pyrex bowl, over a saucepan of simmering water, or microwave. Once it

*FOR THE CHOCOLATE
COATING:*

*7oz (200g) milk chocolate,
broken into small pieces*

has melted, remove from the heat and dip the opposite
end of each bar in the chocolate.

8   Leave to cool on a sheet of greaseproof paper or
non-stick silicon paper.

HOT
ICE-CREAM FOR COLD DAYS
FROM 'CHARLIE AND THE CHOCOLATE FACTORY'

SERVES 6

YOU WILL NEED:

ovenproof dish 10 inch (25 cm)
wide x 2 inch (5 cm) deep

1 Jamaica ginger cake
15oz (420g) tin peach slices
1 litre ice-cream (you probably
won't use all of this)
stem ginger in syrup, drained
and chopped finely (as little or as
much as you dare)
3 egg whites
a pinch of salt
6oz (175g) castor sugar

1 Preheat oven to 230° C (450° F) gas mark 8.

2 Whisk the egg whites with the salt to a stiff snow. Gradually whisk in the sugar until the meringue is very thick and shiny.

3 Cut the Jamaica ginger cake into three horizontal slices. Then cut each slice into a third again.

4 Brush each slice with a little peach syrup.

5 Arrange the nine slices to roughly form a cube in the ovenproof dish.

6 Divide the peaches equally and arrange on top of the cake.

7 Mix the chopped slices of stem ginger into the meringue.

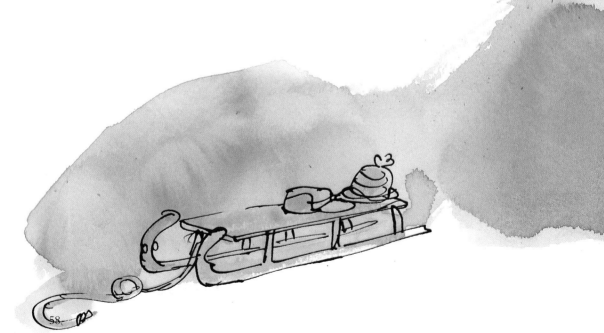

8 Carefully scoop the ice-cream on top of the peaches.

9 Spoon the meringue over the ice-cream, enclosing the cake.

10 Place the pudding in the oven until it has turned golden brown (approx 3-5 minutes).

11 Serve immediately.

NB. If you want to add a *frisson* of excitement to the occasion you can warm up a little brandy in a ladle, set it alight and pour over the pudding. Serve immediately.

HAIR TOFFEE TO MAKE HAIR GROW ON BALD MEN (FOR MUMS TO MAKE ONLY)

FROM 'CHARLIE AND THE CHOCOLATE FACTORY'

YOU WILL NEED:

large saucepan
small greased tin or tray
sugar thermometer
cellophane, foil or greaseproof paper

2oz (50g) unsalted butter
8oz (225g) granulated sugar (cane)
1 tbsp (15ml) warm water
1 tbsp (15ml) white wine vinegar
2 tbsp (30ml) golden syrup
4oz (100g) egg vermicelli, broken in half and cooked

1 Melt the butter in a large, heavy-bottomed pan, stir in the sugar and remove the pan from the heat.

2 Add the water, vinegar and syrup and stir over a low heat until the sugar dissolves. DO NOT allow the mixture to boil.

3 Add the egg vermicelli.

4 Place the sugar thermometer into the pan.

5 Now bring the mixture to boiling point and boil steadily for approx 15-20 minutes until the thermometer reads 152°C (305°F).

6 Pour the toffee into the greased tin and allow to cool. As soon as it is cool enough to handle, lightly grease your hands with butter. Take two forks and scrape up a few strands of vermicelli. Then using your hands, roll the toffee into a small bite-sized mound. Repeat.

7 Place on greased tray and allow to set.

8 Wrap and twist individually in greaseproof paper, kitchen foil or, better still, cellophane, to prevent them from becoming sticky.

NB. Most florists stock cellophane.

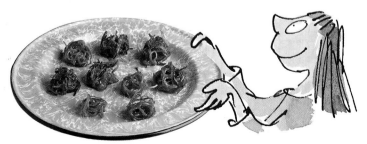

RECIPE LIST

If you've *ever* read Dahl.
If you've *never* read Dahl...

The Roald Dahl Treasury

is the book for you!

Enter the extraordinary world of Roald Dahl in this collection of stories, rhymes, memoirs and even some unpublished poems and letters. Illustrated by a dazzling selection of artists including Raymond Briggs, Babette Cole, Posy Simmonds, Ralph Steadman and, of course, Quentin Blake, this sumptuous volume celebrates some of the most marvellous moments in the life and work of a magical storyteller.

The Roald Dahl Treasury   ISBN 0 224 04691 8   Jonathan Cape